# MR FOSSIL'S DINOSAUR

## L E S S O N S

Valerie Wilding

illustrated by
Kelly Waldek

■SCHOLASTIC

*For my grandson, Kieran Wilding,*
*with all my love*

Scholastic Children's Books,
Commonwealth House, 1–19 New Oxford Street,
London WC1A 1NU, UK

A division of Scholastic Ltd
London ~ New York ~ Toronto ~ Sydney ~ Auckland
Mexico City ~ New Delhi ~ Hong Kong

Published in the UK by Scholastic Ltd, 2002

Text copyright © Valerie Wilding, 2002
Illustrations copyright © Kelly Waldek, 2002

ISBN 0 439 98282 0

Typeset by M Rules
Printed by Cox & Wyman Ltd, Reading, Berks

2 4 6 8 10 9 7 5 3 1

The right of Valerie Wilding and Kelly Waldek to be identified as the
author and illustrator of this work respectively has been asserted by them
in accordance with the Copyright, Designs and Patents Act, 1988.

# Contents

# Welcome To Pickle Hill Primary

Hi! I'm Gordon Budd, and I go to the best school ever—Pickle Hill Primary! What's so special about it? Everything, that's what!

Most schools have a teacher who's a little... strange, right? All our teachers are unusual, to say the least, and they're all totally barmy about their favourite subjects.

When a Pickle Hill Primary teacher begins a lesson, we never know what's going to happen. Will a drawing on the whiteboard come to life? Is someone—or something—waiting for us in the store cupboard? If we boot up the computer, should we stand clear, just in case?

Like to know more? Let me tell you about last Monday morning. 5F's used to having surprise visitors, but even we were staggered by what turned up that day. Take a look!

by **Gordon**

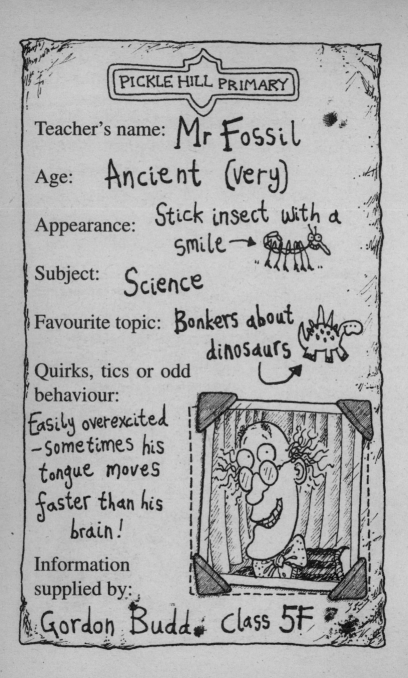

## PICKLE HILL PRIMARY

Teacher's name: **Mr Fossil**

Age: **Ancient (very)**

Appearance: **Stick insect with a smile →**

Subject: **Science**

Favourite topic: **Bonkers about dinosaurs**

Quirks, tics or odd behaviour:

**Easily overexcited — sometimes his tongue moves faster than his brain!**

Information supplied by: **Gordon Budd, class 5F**

# Pongo

Monday started quietly enough in 5F. We got even quieter when the door opened and a new teacher bounced in, dropping his bag and stuff as he kicked the door shut.

"He looks too old to bounce around," I said.

"Shh, Gordon," Tess whispered. "Who is he?"

"I'll tell you," said the teacher, who must have had pretty good hearing. "I'm a clue."

We chanted politely, "Good mor-ning, Mr McClue."

He gave a wide smile, showing absolutely all his teeth.

NO, NO, I'M MR FOSSIL, AND THAT MAKES ME A CLUE TO OUR NEW TOPIC.

That set us thinking.

"Fossils are old bones…"

"Bones of dead things."

"Stone bones."

Mr Fossil said, "Another clue?" He felt in his pocket. "Now where is it? Ah!"

He produced the most amazing miniature skeleton of a —

DINOSAUR!

"Exactly!" said Mr Fossil. "We're going to study dinosaurs. But we need more space." He glanced round. "Push the walls back, please."

We might have known things wouldn't stay normal for long! I shoved against the back wall with Freddie, and once the desks and chairs had moved out of the way – by themselves – we had a vast, empty space.

Mr Fossil passed me the skeleton. "Gordon, put this in the middle of the floor, please." He rubbed his hands together, looking all pleased with himself.

I did it, then whispered to Lizzie, "How did he know my name?"

She shrugged. "It's a mystery to– "

"Ready?" Mr Fossil was hopping about. "Then band stack, everyone!" He stopped and thought for a bit. "Sorry, I mean stand back. Stegosaurus coming up."

We didn't take much notice until Meena pointed to the skeleton and said, "It's growing!" *Then* we moved!

It grew and grew – longer than a desk, longer than a car – until it was ENORMOUS!

"Wow!" said Nita. "Those bones would last my dog at least a year."

"They might even last you a week or two," Tess giggled.

Nita got narked at that, but when I saw what was happening to the skeleton, I dug her in the ribs.

"It's changing," said Hiroko. "It's shimmering."

It was starting to smell, too.

Before us was a living, breathing, *stinking* dinosaur. As if that wasn't amazing enough, it slowly turned its head towards Mr Fossil, and said…

Mr Fossil peered into its eyes and said kindly, "I'm not your mummy, Pongo." He turned to us. "Well?"

We were speechless for a moment, then Will asked the question most of us wanted the answer to.

"Will it eat me?"

Mr Fossil folded his arms. "If you want to know about Pongo, why don't you ask him?"

Will lost his nerve, of course, so Lizzie asked, "Do you want to eat us?"

Pongo swung his head towards her and sniffed. "Are you a bush?"

Lizzie shook her head.

"Are you a leaf?"

"Course not!"

"Then, no thanks," said Pongo. "I'm a – a…"

"Pongo's a herbivore," said Mr Fossil.

**HERBIVORES** by Will Baker

Herbivores only ate plants...
Plant-eating dinosaurs came in all different sizes... Some walked on two legs...
Some on four... 1 2 3 4 Some of the biggest dinosaurs ever were herbivores. Their necks were long enough to reach the treetops.

They had long tails, huge bodies, and very small heads.

"You've got a titchy head," Meena said to the Stegosaurus.

Pongo looked all around, then back between his legs.

"No," he said. "I haven't."

"Haven't what?"

"Haven't got a head."

Lizzie grew impatient. "Of course you have," she said, and tapped him smartly on the forehead. "Here."

14

Pongo went cross-eyed. "I can't see it."

"Mr Fossil," I whispered. "He's a bit, well, daft, isn't he?"

Hiroko snorted. "Pea-brain, if you ask me."

"Not quite as small as a pea," said Mr Fossil. "Pongo's brain is about the size of a large conker."

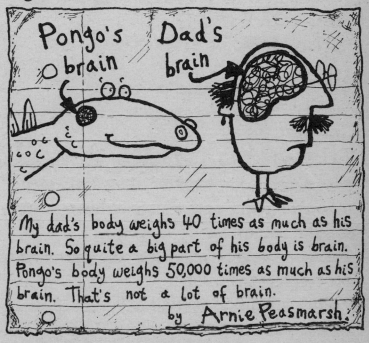

Pongo's brain
Dad's brain

My dad's body weighs 40 times as much as his brain. So quite a big part of his body is brain. Pongo's body weighs 50,000 times as much as his brain. That's not a lot of brain.
                              by Arnie Peasmarsh.

"How did Stegosauruses cope with such small brains?" I asked.

"They didn't need much thinking power," said Mr Fossil. "Pongo! What do you think about?"

The Stegosaurus didn't reply. Lizzie went over to it. "Hey! Pongo! That *is* your name, isn't it?"

"Is it? Yes, that's my name," it said. "Hey Pongo."

"What do you think about all day?"

"Think?" said the Stegosaurus. "I don't think I do think. I eat most of the time. And I watch out for *them*."

"What's them?" asked Meena.

"Them is them, of course." Pongo snorted. "You don't know much, do you?"

Hiroko fell about, which made Meena really mad.

Mr Fossil patted the Stegosaurus, and said, "Pongo means his enemies, the carnivores. A carnivore is a meat-eater, and herbivores were the usual menu."

Freddie laughed. "I hope the carnivores were brighter than Pongo."

"They certainly needed a bit more brain power," said Mr Fossil. "Carnivores had to plan their hunting. Some, like Troodon, had quite large brains for the size of their bodies. They needed them, too."

"Why?" asked Will.

16

Mr Fossil beamed round at us. "If we're going to learn about all these different dinosaurs, we ought to keep a record of them. Who would like to help?"

"Good idea," said Mr Fossil, "so who'll do our very first Dinofax?"

"Me," I said, and dived for the paper tray.

Crash! I really did dive, straight over the rubbish bin. That set everybody off.

"Have a good trip, Gordon?" Tess asked, sniggering.

"More haste, less speed," Meena said. She sounded just like my grandad.

Why does my brain always rush ahead of my body?

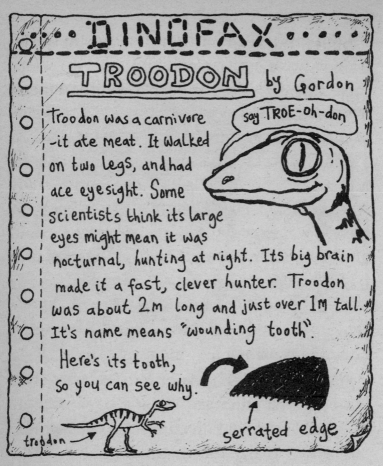

# DINOFAX

## TROODON by Gordon

Troodon was a carnivore -it ate meat. It walked on two legs, and had ace eyesight. Some scientists think its large eyes might mean it was nocturnal, hunting at night. Its big brain made it a fast, clever hunter. Troodon was about 2m long and just over 1m tall. It's name means "wounding tooth".

say TROE-oh-don

Here's its tooth, so you can see why.

troodon →

serrated edge

Pongo was eyeing our bean plants. "Hey! Don't let him eat those," Tess yelled. "They took ages to grow."

"Throw me my backpack, Gordon, quickly," said Mr Fossil.

I grabbed it and went to toss it to him.

"Duck!" yelled Nita. "He'll miss!"

I did miss, but it felt practically empty and Meena hardly grumbled at all.

Mr Fossil opened the bag and pulled out half a dozen leafy cabbages, which he rolled towards Pongo. He's amazing. Mr Fossil, I mean.

Pongo's beaky snout sliced into the cabbages, and before you could say "Stegosaurus", they were gone! He gave a really mega "Buurrrp!", which was so revoltingly stinky you could almost see it in the air. Then he began to turn round and round in circles.

"Wake may!" shouted Mr Fossil. "He's settling down for a snooze. You don't want to be too close when he rolls over!"

Too right. *Down* went the front legs, *down* went the back ones, and *thhhlummp!* went the body as Pongo rolled on his side. He was asleep before he hit the ground.

Tess's forehead wrinkled. "Wake May?" she said. "Who's May?"

I shrugged. Then I twigged. "He meant 'Make way'," I said. "He got the words back to front."

Tess laughed. "If his lessons are this much fun, he can put his head on back to front for all I care!"

# Mighty Mesozoic

"I wonder what's next," said Lizzie. "The Loch Ness monster? Pterodactyls?"

Mr Fossil leapt up. He's even livelier than my gran and she does exercises before breakfast. "First," he said, "let's check what a dinosaur *is* and what it is not." He pulled three little plastic toys from his backpack.

He took the one with wings and tossed it into the air.

"Woooaah!" Lizzie yelled in delight as it swooped and soared above our heads. "It's alive!"

"Yeeow!" Tess bellowed as the creature dived at her. Its long beak yanked out the giant clip that almost held her hair in place.

Mr Fossil reached up and grabbed the creature. "This is a pterosaur." He uncurled his hand and showed us. It was just a toy again. "A pterosaur is a flying reptile, related to the dinosaurs. But it's not a dinosaur. Dinosaurs didn't fly."

Next he tossed the one with flippers into our terrapin tank. It dived underwater, then poked its head up, getting a hard stare from Terry.

Hastily, Mr Fossil plunged his hand in the tank and scooped it out. It was a toy again! "In real life, this plesiosaur would have been hundreds of times bigger than Terry. But big as it was, it was not a dinosaur. It was a sea reptile."

"If the flying one wasn't a dinosaur, and the swimming one wasn't a dinosaur," said Freddie, "what *was* a dinosaur?"

"See this?" Mr Fossil held up the third toy. "No wings. No fins. A dinosaur was a reptile that lived on land."

"Like crocodiles?" Lucy Lee asked.

"A crocodile certainly is a reptile," said Mr Fossil, "and it's another relation of the dinosaurs." He wiped the eraser over the whiteboard, which seemed a bit daft, as there was nothing to rub out. But instead, a drawing of a crocodile appeared! Another wipe and there was a dinosaur.

Both creatures walked across the board! Will moved back, just in case they walked right off the edge. I don't blame him. You can never tell what's going to happen in this place.

Mr Fossil asked, "Can anyone spot an important difference between them?"

"I can," said Tess, who's always fast with an answer (but not always right).

Dinosaur    Crocodile

CROCODILE LEGS STICK OUT AT THE SIDES AND DINOSAUR LEGS ARE LIKE ELEPHANT LEGS— STRAIGHT UNDERNEATH THEIR BODIES.

This time she was right.

"Exactly so." Mr Fossil looked pleased (not as pleased as Tess). "Those legs have a lot of weight to support."

"Let's see some more dinosaurs," shouted Arnie Peasmarsh.

"Yeah," said Lizzie, "killer dinos!" Honestly, that girl loves blood and gore.

Tess was still watching the drawings march up and down. "Were crocodiles around at the same time as dinosaurs?" she asked.

"Let's find out," said Mr Fossil. "Where shall we start?"

"The beginning?" Hiroko said, cheekily.

Mr Fossil gave her a toothy grin. "OK." He looked at the marker pens. "Blue, I think."

The blue pen stood on end, the cap flipped off and it wrote across the bottom of the board – all by itself.

"I wish I could do that," said Meena. "My homework could be done while I watch TV."

"It already is," said Hiroko, who was sure that Meena's dad did everything for her.

THE BEGINNING
4,600 mya

"What's a mya?" asked Carrie Marsh.

"I know," I said. Tess gave me a look. She reckons I spend my life buried in CD-ROMs and encyclopaedias. "It stands for 'million years ago'."

"Spot on!" said Mr Fossil. "4,600 million years ago is when scientists believe the story of our planet began – the origin of Earth. Keep watching and you'll see the march of time."

Words and figures appeared one after the other until they stretched right across the whiteboard. When the board was full, the timeline scrolled to the left and more came into view from the right. Shellfish soon appeared, followed by fish, and then Lizzie jumped up.

"Here's the interesting stuff," she said. "Reptiles!" She snapped her hands together, like a crocodile, at Will's left ear.

Mr Fossil smiled. "I think you'll find the *really* interesting stuff is just about to appear."

And it did!

The dinosaurs moved left, then came the mammals, followed by humans, and there we were, at today.

"Oh!" Meena stuck out her bottom lip. "Can't we go back to the Mesa … Meso…"

"Mesozoic," I said.

Lizzie looked confused. "What's the Mesozoic?"

"If you hadn't been busy doing crocodile impressions," said Mr Fossil, "you'd have seen that the Mesozoic era was the time of the dinosaurs. 'Mesozoic' means 'middle life' and it began 251 million years ago and ended 65 million years ago. It's divided into three sections. The early part was the Triassic period, then the Jurassic, and finally the Cretaceous."

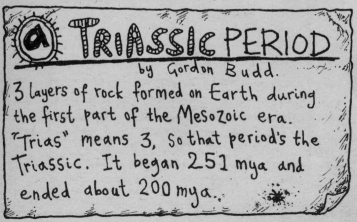

TRIASSIC PERIOD
by Gordon Budd.
3 layers of rock formed on Earth during the first part of the Mesozoic era. "Trias" means 3, so that period's the Triassic. It began 251 mya and ended about 200 mya.

If I'd been alive then, I might have met **HERRERASAURUS!**

Say hare-AIR-a-SORE-us

This is one of the earliest-known dinosaurs. It had sharp teeth and ate meat, so it was a carnivore. Those large strong jaws could open really wide and grip its victim so hard there was no escape. Yikes!

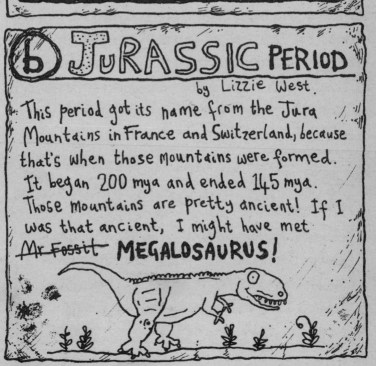

# ⓑ JURASSIC PERIOD

by Lizzie West

This period got its name from the Jura Mountains in France and Switzerland, because that's when those mountains were formed. It began 200 mya and ended 145 mya. Those mountains are pretty ancient! If I was that ancient, I might have met ~~Mr Fossil~~ **MEGALOSAURUS!**

This dinosaur was 9m long and weighed a ton, so you can see why it was called Megalosaurus, which means "great lizard". Look at those teeth and claws. It was a killer! Cool!

# © CRETACEOUS PERIOD
by Will Baker

The word "Cretaceous" comes from the Latin word for chalk. In this period, chalky layers built up. How? Zillions of shells piled up on the sea beds and gradually turned into chalk. The Cretaceous period began 145 mya and ended 65 mya. This is what I might have met if I'd been around that long ago.

**Kritosaurus** (KRIT-oh-SORE-us) was almost as long as Megalosaurus, but about 3 times as heavy! Its head was a bit lumpy-bumpy as if someone had thumped it. And it had teeth! Rows and rows of them! It was a plant-eater, but I still wouldn't have liked to meet it.

Hiroko frowned. "What was it like in the Mesozoic era?"

Mr Fossil looked around at us. "What do you think?"

He went to the wall and pulled our world map down. Right down. In fact, he pulled it off the wall and laid it on the floor.

"Hey! It's changing!" said Arnie Peasmarsh.

It was! All the countries swirled, like a whirlpool, then settled again.

I stared. "All the land is one big blob."

"That's right," said Mr Fossil. "Let me introduce you to the world in Triassic times. That blob is called Pangaea."

No sooner had he said this than the sea flowed into odd parts of Pangaea, and the blob began to split up and move apart.

"The land's moving again," said Lucy. "Why is it doing that?"

"Land moves all the time," said Mr Fossil.

Will gasped in fright and grabbed the kids either side of him.

"It's OK," said Freddie. "It's not moving now."

SOLID AS A ROCK.

SSH! YOU'LL WAKE PONGO.

Mr Fossil shook his head. "The continents are always moving. Some are drifting apart, and others are moving together, but only by a few centimetres a year. Don't worry – we won't suddenly bump into Africa!"

The map settled again. "Ah," he said, "here's the world in the Jurassic period. Next we'll see what it was like in the Cretaceous."

# The MESOZOIC WORLD

by Hiroko Tanaka

**1.** By **Triassic** times, all the land on Earth had joined together in one blob called Pangaea (Pan-JEE-a).
This is a supercontinent.
"Pangaea" means "all earth".

**2.** In the **Jurassic** the land was split into two big blobs.
This one was called Laurasia.
This one was Gondwana.
Two supercontinents!

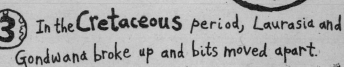

**3.** In the **Cretaceous** period, Laurasia and Gondwana broke up and bits moved apart.
Laurasia split into North America, Europe and North Asia. Gondwana became South America, Africa, India, Antarctica and Australia.

"The Cretaceous world is much more like ours today, isn't it?" said Carrie Marsh.

"Bet it wasn't," said Lizzie. "Bet the whole of the Mesozoic era was wild and dangerous."

"Wild's not the word!" said Mr Fossil. "Want to see?"

"Yes!" Lizzie shouted.

Mr Fossil's eyes sparkled, and he threw his arms wide. "Then let's lake a took!" He stopped. "What did I say?"

"Let's take a look!" we shouted.

"Let's not," said Will.

"How can you be scared of dinosaurs?" Tess demanded. "They're all dead!"

Will eyed the sleeping Stegosaurus. "Oh, yes?"

"Oh, Pongo's more like a – a teacher's pet," said Tess. "I mean all the *real* dinosaurs – they died out years ago."

"I *know* that," Will said, looking at her as if she was mad. "But this is Pickle Hill!"

# Curtains for 5F

"Curtains closed, I think," said Mr Fossil.

"I'll do it," I said, and climbed over a couple of chairs. I never made it. Somehow my foot got wedged in the bin and by the time I'd sorted myself out the curtains had closed. On their own.

"Telly time," Will said happily.

But once the chairs had rearranged themselves, we realized we weren't going to watch TV. They faced the window. Pongo caused a slight traffic jam as we sat down, but Mr Fossil said we should let him sleep, because he was less trouble that way. Anyway, who wanted to take a chance on waking a dozing dinosaur? Not me!

Mr Fossil made a grand gesture at the curtains and cried, "Open, sez me!"

Whoosh! The curtains swished back.

The windows reached from floor to ceiling, and instead of our usual view, the ground sloped down to a shallow river.

"Wow!" I said. "What's happened?"

Mr Fossil smiled. "You wanted to see the Mesozoic era. Out there," he said, "it's the Triassic period. Plenty of plants here, near the river, but inland it's just desert."

Hiroko pointed to the left. "Palm trees!"

"Not exactly," said Mr Fossil. "Look again."

He was right. They were a cross between a palm tree and a fern.

"Not palm trees," said Mr Fossil. "Tree ferns."

Will got enthusiastic about some tall trees in the distance, with beautiful, dark, curving branches. "I've got one of those in my garden!" he shouted. "It's a monkey-puzzle!"

MONKEY-PUZZLES ARE GOOD FOOD FOR DINOSAURS.

Will shrank back. "D-dinosaurs?"

"Scaredy-cat!" Meena giggled and got up. "I'll make sure the window's shut tight." She reached for the handle.

DINOSAUR!

Meena shot backwards across the room, fell against Pongo and sat sprawled on his great tummy. Her mouth opened and closed, with no sound coming out.

"It's a bit small," Lizzie muttered. "Not much taller than Mr Fossil."

The dinosaur wandered down the slope, so we got up to look closer. I had to help Will – his legs were wobbling.

"That's Coelophysis," said Mr Fossil, gazing at it in admiration. "What a beauty! See those long, narrow jaws? It's a predator – a meat-eater – and most predators were quite small in the Triassic. But see, it's not alone."

There was a whole pack of them!

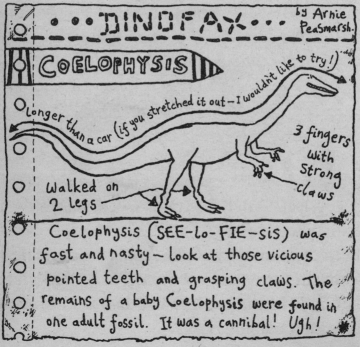

•••DINOFAX••• by Arnie Peasmarsh.

COELOPHYSIS

longer than a car (if you stretched it out – I wouldn't like to try!)

3 fingers with strong claws

Walked on 2 legs

Coelophysis (SEE-Lo-FIE-sis) was fast and nasty – look at those vicious pointed teeth and grasping claws. The remains of a baby Coelophysis were found in one adult fossil. It was a cannibal! Ugh!

"So there weren't any big dinosaurs here?" Will asked hopefully. He was still eyeing the Coelophysis, which in turn was eyeing a crocodile-like creature crawling out of the river.

"There's always the Plateosaurus," said Mr Fossil.

"Can we see one?" asked Freddie.

"If you look up."

Once we'd stopped screaming, Mr Fossil started to explain that the Plateosaurus was a plant-eater, but his words tumbled over themselves. "It needed fountains of mood to keep that enormous body going," he gabbled. "I mean, moontains of – oh, I'm so thrilled to see it I don't know what I mean – but it wouldn't eat you."

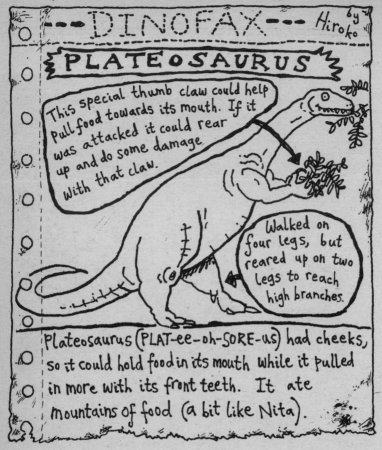

**PLATEOSAURUS**

This special thumb claw could help pull food towards its mouth. If it was attacked it could rear up and do some damage with that claw.

Walked on four legs, but reared up on two legs to reach high branches.

Plateosaurus (PLAT-ee-oh-SORE-us) had cheeks, so it could hold food in its mouth while it pulled in more with its front teeth. It ate mountains of food (a bit like Nita).

"So Triassic dinosaurs were mainly smallish meat-eaters, and plant-eaters the size of buses," said Freddie. "Were there bigger ones in the Jurassic?"

Mr Fossil bounded to the window, and whooshed his hands again.

Swish! The curtains closed. Swoosh! Open!

"Wooah!" This time we *all* shot backwards across the room.

Mr Fossil nearly burst his shirt buttons laughing. "Come back," he said, "you're quite safe."

Hiroko got her breath back first. "That's five times the size of the Plateosaurus!"

"And isn't it wonderful!" said Mr Fossil. "The Apatosaurus is a plant-eater and, with a tummy that big to fill, it has to eat nearly all day."

Nita groaned enviously. "Lucky thing."

"I think it'd better move," said Mr Fossil. "There's an Allosaurus crossing the river. Now *that* is a meat-eater."

"Apatosaurus would make a pretty large meal," said Nita. "How big is it, sir?"

"Longer than as a tennis court," Mr Fossil said, "and as it weighed over 30 tons and could squash most meat-eaters, I don't think it's likely to be dinner for any of them. Mind you, the Allosaurus would happily rip a few bites out of one of those legs."

Oh, yuck! He's as bad as Lizzie! She was gazing at the Allosaurus the way Nita stares at a doughnut – as if it was the most wonderful thing she'd seen for days.

"Look at that huge head," she murmured.

"Magnificent!" Mr Fossil agreed. "Those teeth must be 10 centimetres long."

Penny White gulped. "Like daggers – and it's got a whole mouthful of them!"

40

The Allosaurus suddenly darted at the Apatosaurus and sank its teeth and front claws into a hind leg. The Apatosaurus roared and lashed its tail round, catching the Allosaurus on the side of the head. The Allosaurus took off back across the river.

"Wow! That was fast!" I said.

"Big, strong legs," said Mr Fossil. "Meat-eaters need speed." He turned. "Yes, Will?"

"Can't we just look at the trees and flowers and little creatures, sir?"

"Actually," said Mr Fossil, "there aren't any flowers. Flowers – and bees – didn't arrive until the Cretaceous period."

"I noticed there weren't any flowers, sir," I said.

Tess mouthed, "Creep!" at me from behind Mr Fossil's back.

I ignored her and went on, "But there's something else missing, and I can't think what."

"If you do some work on Mesozoic wildlife for the display board," Mr Fossil said, "it will probably come to you. Will could help." He turned to Tess. "You, too. Perhaps you could all creep off together and get on with it." She went scarlet.

All through the Mesozoic there were 🐢 and creatures a lot like 🐊 in the rivers. 🐸 and 🦎 were all over the place, and made tasty meals for some 🦕. In the Jurassic, you would see 🌿 and 🌳 everywhere on the ground. In the air you would see 🦋, and the first 🐦 There were insects, too, like 🪰 and dung 🪲 (ugh!) and 🐛. There were little furry 🐁 who mostly came out at night. Otherwise they'd be tasty dinners

for 🦕. Plant life went mad in the Cretaceous and the first 🌼 appeared. There were even magnolia 🌳 and Will's got one in his garden. Along came 🐜 and 🐝 and 🦋 so it must have looked really pretty, apart from the 🦕. And 🐛 – they were Cretaceous creatures, too!

by Gordon, Will and Tess

And I realized what else was missing. All through the Mesozoic there was NO GRASS!

by Gordon

dinosaurs →
beetles →
ferns →
turtles →

shrew-like mammals → lizards →

# Tails, with knobs on

After lunch, we found Mr Fossil, feet on his desk, eyes shut. Pongo was still snoring.

"Ah, sweet," said Meena. "Gordon! What are you doing?"

"Having a closer look at Pongo." I touched one of his tail spikes.

AWESOME! NEARLY TWICE AS LONG AS MY ARM! WHAT ARE THEY FOR?

IF I HAD A TAIL LIKE THAT, I'D SWING IT, LIKE THIS. AND I'D STAB ANY BIG OLD DINOSAUR THAT DARED TO COME NEAR.

"Exactly right."

That made us jump! We hadn't seen Mr Fossil move.

"Pongo's tail is well-suited for putting off attackers," said Mr Fossil, "but what would you do if you had a tail like Gordon's?"

Huh? They all turned and stared, then shrieked with laughter and pointed. I looked behind me and saw – a tail! I spun round, and so did the tail. It was a very long tail, too. Everyone bolted out of the way. I spun round and round trying to see where it began.

Hiroko hooted. "I had a cat that did that – chased its own tail!"

Its own tail? I bent down and looked between my legs. There was no doubt about it – that tail was attached to me!

I found I could wave it about as 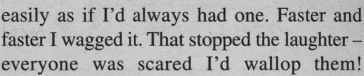 easily as if I'd always had one. Faster and faster I wagged it. That stopped the laughter – everyone was scared I'd wallop them!

Suddenly, my tail moved so fast it made a noise like a whip. *Crack!*

That was a bit scary!

But soon we were all laughing again when I hooked my tail round Nita's lunch box and dragged it across the room. She chased after it angrily, but as she ran, *she* grew a tail. That slowed her down.

"Hey! This is heavy!" she shouted. "Help me, someone!"

Nobody moved. It was my turn to laugh when I saw why. *Everyone* had tails!

Mr Fossil pulled up a chair and sat with his feet on Pongo's tummy. They moved up and down with every giant Stegosaurus breath. "Can you find out how dinosaurs might have used those tails?"

Dinosaur Tails...

@ My tail was 10m long and very thin at the end. **Diplodocus** had one like this and could crack it like a whip to scare off enemies or hurt them. Some scientists think that Diplodocus held its head low when it walked so that its neck and tail balanced each other. That must have been quite a sight — from head to tail, Diplodocus was longer than two buses put together! BY GORDON

ⓑ Saying **Euoplocephalus** gets my tongue in a knot. It's "yoo-OP-lo-KEF-al-us". That means "well-armoured head", but it was well-armoured

PTO

everywhere, except its tummy. Mr Fossil gave me a Euoplocephalus tail. It was like a club, and the knobby bone on the end weighed 30kg! That's like 12 bags of potatoes. Imagine that hammering against your shin! If I was a dinosaur, I'd let my attacker come up behind me, then **WHAM!** I'd bash his brains in. Bet that's what Euoplocephalus did. by LIZZIE

© My tail looked pretty ordinary, until I realised I could sit on it. Cathetosaurus had a tail like this. Its name means "upright lizard", which seems daft, when it's obvious it had four legs. But if it wanted to eat from the treetops, it could have reared up and sat upright on its chunky tail! Comfy! by Freddie Field

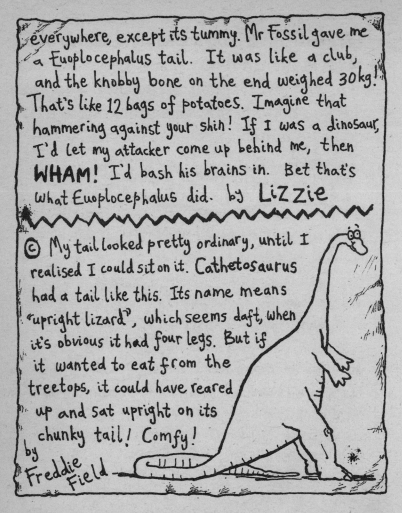

"So tail spikes and clubs weren't really for attacking," said Meena. "Dinosaurs used them to defend themselves."

I nodded. "A bit like Euoplocephalus's armour. Why didn't all dinosaurs have armour?"

"The real giants didn't need it," said Mr Fossil.

"You bet they didn't!" Lizzie stamped a foot down, hard. "They could crush a little old meat-eater!" She stamped the other foot. "Squelch!"

"And some of the smaller dinosaurs were fast movers," Mr Fossil continued, "so their defence was running away."

"Like my sister when she sees a spider," said Nita. "But I suppose they couldn't have run so fast if they'd had a tail as heavy as Lizzie's – I mean Euoplocephalus's."

EUOPLOCEPHALUS DIDN'T NEED TO RUN. IF IT WAS ATTACKED, IT COULD SIMPLY SINK DOWN ON THE GROUND TO PROTECT ITS TUMMY, WHICH WASN'T ARMOURED. EVERY EXPOSED PART, EVEN ITS EYE-LIDS, WAS COVERED IN BONY ARMOUR.

BONY EYELIDS! I CAN SEE WHY ITS NAME MEANS "WELL-ARMOURED HEAD".

Mr Fossil told us to sit down.

"With these tails?" said Hiroko.

"What tails?" he replied.

I spun round. My tail had gone. So had everyone else's!

Mr Fossil crossed to the overhead projector. The light came on, though I swear he never touched it, and the screen rolled down.

"Let's see an armoured dinosaur from the same family as Euoplocephalus," he said, happily clapping his hands. "They're the amazing ankylosaurs! Kids, I want you to eat Medmontonia!"

Nita looked interested. "Eat what, sir?"

"Eat?" he said, puzzled. Then his face cleared. "Sorry – I meant *meet* Edmontonia."

"Oh," said Nita.

"Sir!" Hiroko said. "You've forgotten the transparent sheet!"

Mr Fossil smiled his wide smile. "I don't need one."

He obviously didn't, because the picture came up on the screen as clear as anything, and what's more, it moved!

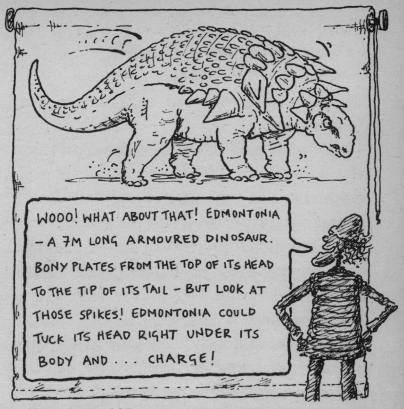

WOOO! WHAT ABOUT THAT! EDMONTONIA
– A 7M LONG ARMOURED DINOSAUR.
BONY PLATES FROM THE TOP OF ITS HEAD
TO THE TIP OF ITS TAIL – BUT LOOK AT
THOSE SPIKES! EDMONTONIA COULD
TUCK ITS HEAD RIGHT UNDER ITS
BODY AND . . . CHARGE!

"I wonder if I could do that," I said. I got up, tucked my head under my body, and tried to look at my bottom. I'd have been all right if Freddie hadn't helped me. He forced my head just that bit too far and – whoops! – over I went.

"Very clever, Gordon," said Mr Fossil.

I don't think he meant it.

# Toothy pegs

There was a great snort behind us. We all jumped, but it was only Pongo stirring.

Lizzie tapped him on the nose. "Wake up!"

His piggy eyes blinked open. "Hello, Mummy."

Lizzie laughed so much she nearly fell over. "I'm not your mummy," she said. "I've come to look at your armour."

"My arm or what?" said Pongo.

"Your armour." Lizzie pointed to the diamond-shaped bony plates running down his back. "You're well armoured."

Pongo peered round at his great body. "I'm well legged," he said. "Where are my arms?"

"No, you're well ar… Never mind." Lizzie rolled her eyes. "Sir, Pongo is well armoured, isn't he?"

"Scientists thought the same as you," said

Mr Fossil, "that the plates were for protection. In fact, Stegosaurus means 'roof lizard'. Perhaps the person who named it thought those bony plates were like tiles, which certainly do protect roofs."

Lizzie licked her finger and drew a one in the air, as if she'd scored.

She hadn't.

"But," Mr Fossil continued, "scientists now believe those plates were used to help Stegosaurus stay at the right temperature. They think its heart pumped blood through the skin covering the plates – though nobody's absolutely sure."

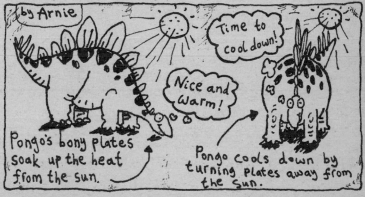

"The other possibility," said Mr Fossil, "is that the plates changed colour when blood was forced into them."

"A yummy shade of pink, I think," said Penny.

Arnie snorted. "That would attract the girls, all right!"

Mr Fossil smiled. "I think that was the general idea."

Pongo lumbered to his feet and yawned. Lizzie tried to peer inside, but nearly got her nose sliced off as Pongo's mouth snapped shut. "I can't see any teeth," she said. "His mouth is just like a beak."

"Pongo does have some teeth," said Mr Fossil. "Let's have a look."

The Stegosaurus blinked lazily. "Goodbye, Pongo," he said, and began to shimmer. Three seconds later, he was just a skeleton. Two seconds later, Mr Fossil held a skull, and the rest of Pongo had disappeared.

The smell hadn't.

"I wish I could do that," said Hiroko.

"What?" asked Meena. "Disappear?"

"No," said Hiroko. "Make annoying people disappear."

"And who d'you mean by that?"

They'd have gone on till home time, if Mr Fossil hadn't interrupted.

LOOK AT THESE CHOPPERS! PONGO'S BEAK SLICES OFF THE EXTREMELY TOUGH LEAVES HE LIKES TO EAT, AND THE BACK TEETH CHOP IT UP READY TO SWALLOW.

THOSE TEETH AREN'T VERY SHARP.

HE WOULDN'T NEED SHARP TEETH IF HE DIDN'T EAT MEAT.

"Carnivores needed quite different teeth," said Mr Fossil. "Gordon, there's a tooth in the front pocket of my backpack. Could you get it, please?"

I groped round the bottom of the pocket. There was nothing that felt like a tooth. Then I checked into the corners where fluffy bits get caught. "No tooth here," I said. "Only this."

"Any idea what makes that tooth perfect for a meat-eater?" Mr Fossil asked.

"Dead sharp," said Lizzie. "That could bite into live flesh, like this." And she snapped her teeth and shook her head, like a dog shaking a rat.

"It's big," said Will. "Big and strong. And horrible."

Now I'd got used to the idea that the huge object I was holding was a tooth, I looked closer and ran my finger down the side of it. "It's rough," I said. "I thought it would be smooth."

Mr Fossil nodded. "The edge of each tooth is serrated," he said, "and when a predator gets a mouthful of flesh and shakes it, rather like Lizzie's little demonstration just now…"

She bowed, but we ignored her.

"…the teeth cut right through the meat."

"Like a saw?" asked Carrie.

"Exactly," said Mr Fossil.

"Or a steak knife," said Nita. "I'm hungry."

Mr Fossil laughed. "Then be thankful you don't have teeth like Plateosaurus, otherwise you'd go home to a meal of leaves."

Tess ruffled her hair, a sure sign that she was thinking. (It might have helped her brain, but it didn't do much for her hair.)

SO DINOSAURS' TEETH WERE SPECIALLY SUITED TO THE FOOD THEY ATE, RIGHT?

EXACTLY. THERE WERE EVEN DIFFERENT SORTS OF TEETH FOR DIFFERENT PLANT-EATERS.

"Look at some more teeth," said Mr Fossil, "and work out which dinosaur might have had them, and what it might have eaten." He tossed his backpack to Tess. "They're in the front pocket."

I was just about to tell him that there definitely weren't any more teeth in the bag, when – wouldn't you know it? – Tess pulled out a whole handful!

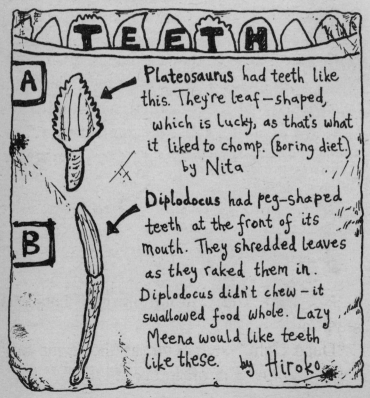

TEETH

A

Plateosaurus had teeth like this. They're leaf-shaped, which is lucky, as that's what it liked to chomp. (Boring diet.) by Nita

B

Diplodocus had peg-shaped teeth at the front of its mouth. They shredded leaves as they raked them in. Diplodocus didn't chew – it swallowed food whole. Lazy Meena would like teeth like these. by Hiroko

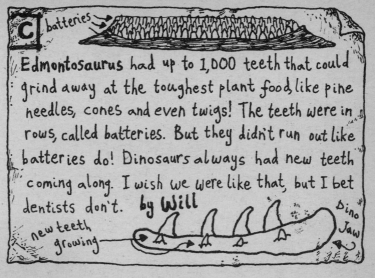

C batteries

Edmontosaurus had up to 1,000 teeth that could grind away at the toughest plant food, like pine needles, cones and even twigs! The teeth were in rows, called batteries. But they didn't run out like batteries do! Dinosaurs always had new teeth coming along. I wish we were like that, but I bet dentists don't. **by Will**

new teeth growing

Dino Jaw

Mr Fossil asked Freddie to open his mouth. "Everyone look at Freddie's teeth," he said. "You'll see that some of them are suitable for biting, and some for chewing and grinding. That's because Freddie is neither a herbivore nor a carnivore."

"What is he then?" asked Tess, peering into his mouth.

"He's an omnivore – he'll eat anything," said Mr Fossil.

"No, that's Nita," Hiroko snorted. "Nita eats anything."

"Dead right," said Nita, as the home bell clanged. "And I'm off to eat my tea."

# Fossils and footprints

"I know that people dig up dinosaur bones," I said at the start of Wednesday's lesson, "and that they're fossils, but what I don't know is how the bones got to be fossils in the first place. Why didn't they just rot away?"

"Or get eaten?" added Nita.

"Most did," said Mr Fossil. "Animals might eat the flesh, the rest would rot and the bones would crumble until nothing was left."

"So how come some skeletons last for millions of years?" asked Meena.

"With the help of good old planet Earth." Mr Fossil flipped open his backpack. We moved aside, just in case. "As it happens," he said, "fossils are what we're going to find out about today." He took out a plastic dinosaur and laid it on his hand so the tail flopped and hung down. It looked like a *real* dead dino.

"Let's imagine this dinosaur's just died in a rock fall and tumbled into the edge of a river. Excuse me, Terry." He tossed the dinosaur into the terrapin tank and we crouched down to watch. Lizzie went right up close.

The dinosaur slowly sank into soft mud. "Keep watching," said Mr Fossil, as water washed over it. "Here it goes, it's going ... gone! Fossilisation begins! Mind-blowing! We'll come back for another look in a few minutes. Now who could do a piece for the display board showing this incredible process? Wizzie and Lill, I think!"

We fell about.

# FOSSIL FORMATION

by Lizzie, and Will. (we think he meant us!)

Over millions and millions of years mud turns into rock. Minerals in the rock seep into minute holes in the bones. The minerals become hard, too, and there you have it — a fossilized skeleton.

"Bones aren't the only dinosaur fossils that have been found," said Mr Fossil. "Any idea what other sorts of fossils there are?"

"Ancient teachers?" Hiroko whispered in my ear, which made me snort.

"I don't mean to be rude, Mr Fossil," said Arnie, "but doesn't 'fossil' mean 'old bone'? So what else could there be?"

THE WORD "FOSSIL" COMES FROM A LATIN WORD MEANING "DUG UP". SO IT COULD BE ANY PART OF A DINOSAUR BODY THAT WE WERE LUCKY ENOUGH TO FIND. NOT JUST BONES, MAYBE SOMETHING DIFFERENT...

"What does he mean, 'something different'?" wondered Meena.

"Something not the same, of course," said Hiroko.

"I know!" said Lizzie. "Dinosaur teeth!"

"And what about claws?" said Lizzie, slashing at Carrie Marsh, who screamed.

# COOL CLAWS

## by Lizzie West

Three of **Diplodocus's** back toes had claws. Perhaps they stopped it slipping down slopes — that's a lot of weight to fall down a hill!

But if you want to see some dead dangerous claws, have a look at these!

This belongs to **Deinonychus**. One of those claws could fold up off the ground when Deinonychus ran, so it didn't go blunt. Then it could SLASH its victim and RIP its guts out — what a weapon!

But the scariest claws I've seen belong to **Deinocheirus**! →

Deinocheirus means "terrible hand". The only part that's been found is a pair of huge arms, 2.5m long. The curved claws are 25cm long — that's nearly a whole ruler length!

my arm

64

> Deinocheirus could have been the most
> incredibly gigantic meat-eater. Or it might
> have been just a lazy dinosaur that sat
> around in the middle of the forest using its
> long arms to pull food towards it. That
> would be a swizz. I'd rather it was the most
> humungous, most vicious, deadliest dinosaur
> ever discovered.

"OK, fossilized claws and teeth," said Mr Fossil. "Anything else?"

"I know something," said Meena. "My mum says some dinosaurs had feathers."

"Fossil traces of dinosaur feathers certainly have been found," agreed Mr Fossil, "but we don't know if they were to keep them warm, or to make them look attractive to their mates."

"So did feathered dinosaurs turn into birds?" Meena asked.

Everyone laughed.

Instead of answering, Mr Fossil went into the store cupboard. There was a loud flapping noise. "Quietly, now," we heard him say, and then out he came.

That shut us up!

BACK IN THE 19th CENTURY, THE FOSSIL OF THIS ARCHAEOPTERYX WAS DISCOVERED. YES, IT HAD FEATHERS. BUT IS IT A BIRD?

SEE THOSE TEETH? AND THE CLAWS? WHAT ABOUT THE STIFF, BONY TAIL? THEY'RE ALL FEATURES OF A DINOSAUR.

ARCHAEOPTERYX IS A SORT OF CROSS BETWEEN A BIRD AND A DINOSAUR — IT MIGHT EVEN HAVE BEEN ABLE TO FLY A LITTLE.

BECAUSE OF THIS SORT OF DISCOVERY, MOST EXPERTS HAVE COME TO AGREE THAT OVER MILLIONS OF YEARS BIRDS EVOLVED FROM SMALL MEAT-EATING DINOSAURS. GIVES ME SHIVERS WHEN I LOOK AT VULTURES!

The Archaeopteryx spotted Terry, and opened and closed its beak, looking horribly greedy. Mr Fossil quickly put it back in the cupboard.

"Have you thought of any other types of fossils?" he asked.

We were stuck for ideas. What else could be fossilized?

"Dinosaur feet?" Meena said hesitantly.

We cracked up, but Mr Fossil surprised us.

"Meena's not so wrong," he said. "People might not have found actual feet, but they've certainly found fossilized footprints."

"Eh? How can you have a fossil of a footprint?" Freddie asked. "A footprint's not something you can pick up. It's empty."

"Bones and teeth and claws are called body fossils," said Mr Fossil. "But there are other fossils, called trace fossils."

"Ah – because they're of traces of dinosaurs," I said.

"Exactly, Gordon, and footprints are trace fossils so, you see, Meena's idea was a good one, after all."

"But what use are footprints?" asked Lucy Lee.

"The only way we can ever find out about dinosaurs is by examining the traces they leave behind," Mr Fossil explained, "and every trace, whether it's bone or tooth or just a footprint, tells us something."

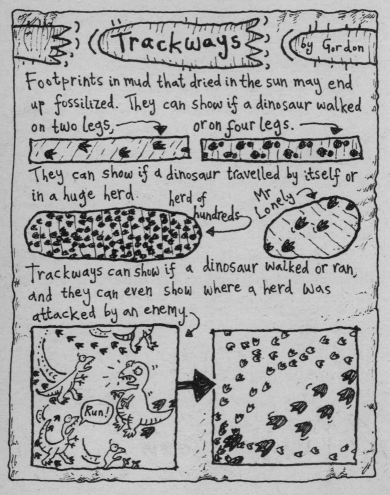

Trackways — by Gordon

Footprints in mud that dried in the sun may end up fossilized. They can show if a dinosaur walked on two legs, or on four legs.

They can show if a dinosaur travelled by itself or in a huge herd.

herd of hundreds

Mr Lonely

Trackways can show if a dinosaur walked or ran, and they can even show where a herd was attacked by an enemy.

Run!

Meena looked quite smug about her foot idea, but laughed her head off when Arnie asked, "What about fossilized dung?"

"That's poo to you," Hiroko whispered.

Arnie stuck out his tongue. "Poo to you, too!"

"I've got one thing to say to you, young Arnie," said Mr Fossil. "Coprolites!"

Arnie looked up. "Eh?"

Mr Fossil fished in his bag.

THESE ARE COPROLITES — FOSSILIZED DINOSAUR POO. BITS OF FOSSILIZED FOOD IN THE POO TELL US WHAT THE DINOSAUR ATE. EVEN THE SHAPE GIVES US INFORMATION — IT TELLS US WHAT THE DINOSAUR'S INTESTINES WERE LIKE.

POO!

I THINK THE SMELL HAS FADED AFTER A HUNDRED MILLION YEARS.

He felt in his bag again, and put a few stones on the table, some as big as apples.

Penny White looked closer. "They're shiny." She picked one up and ran her fingertips over it. "This feels as if it's been polished. It's beautiful."

"Are they fossilized eyeballs?" Lizzie asked.

Penny dropped the stone and Meena nearly fainted.

"Don't be stupid," said Tess. "They're baby dinosaur poos!"

"No, they're not," said Mr Fossil. "But they do come from inside a dinosaur."

"Eeyuck!" Penny wiped her hands on Carrie's sweatshirt.

Mr Fossil held up a stone. "Gastrolith!"

"Bless you!" said Tess.

HERBIVORES WITH TEETH LIKE DIPLODOCUS COULDN'T CHEW THEIR FOOD. BUT ALL THAT VEGETATION HAD TO BE BROKEN DOWN SOMEHOW. GASTROLITHS — OR STOMACH STONES — WERE THE ANSWER.

"How did they work?" I asked.

"I'll show you." Mr Fossil tossed me a marker pen. "Draw a plant-eater with its stomach and intestines."

I laughed. "I can't."

He grinned. "You're doing it."

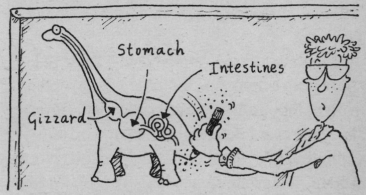

When I looked I couldn't believe it. There was my hand finishing a pretty good drawing of a dinosaur, if I say so myself.

Mr Fossil passed me some rough stones. "Hold these to its mouth," he said.

I knew better than to say "I can't" this time, so I did it. The mouth opened, took the stone from me and swallowed it!

"Cool!" said Freddie. "Can I have a go?"

He put a stone in. Then Tess and Arnie had a go.

I held up a branch, which Mr Fossil produced from his bottomless backpack, where else? The dinosaur raked in the leaves, swallowed them, and we watched them go down to the gizzard. There, the stones began to rub together, like marbles in a bag. The leaves were slowly ground down into a mush. That was pushed through to the stomach, and Mr Fossil said we'd better get rid of the dinosaur before it went any further.

"I'll rub it off," said Nita, diving for the eraser. But she didn't need to. With a burp, the dinosaur was gone.

"Sir, those stones were rough and horrible," said Carrie. "They weren't smooth and shiny like the ones you showed us first. Why not?"

"Anybody thought about that?" asked Mr Fossil.

I had, actually, but I didn't have an answer.

Will did. "Was it because the stones start off rough and get worn smooth?"

"Spot on, Will," said Mr Fossil. "When they were too smooth to be any use, the dinosaur simply vomited them up. It's something that chickens and some other birds still do today."

"I wish I hadn't touched those stones," Penny moaned. "I feel ill."

"That reminds me," said Mr Fossil. "Guess what else scientists have found."

I groaned. "Don't tell me they've found dinosaur sick."

Mr Fossil made a face. "Let's call it fossilized vomit. It was found in Spain, and it contained birds' bones." He went over to Terry's tank. "Aha, I think our fossils are ready. Come and take another look. Of course," he added, "all this should really take several million years, not twenty minutes or so."

We gathered round the tank. Terry's eyes followed every movement.

"Imagine, class, that millions of years are

passing. The Earth's surface shifts…"

Terry scuttled into the water as the rock he was on heaved up and a mini-mountain appeared behind him. The water level dropped, and the mud-rock containing our fossil was left bare.

"Now imagine millions more years passing. Rain and wind gradually wear away the layers covering our fossil. Freddie, have a blow."

Freddie blew into the tank.

And it happened – right before our eyes! I don't mean the millions of years, but the rock gradually wore away until bones appeared.

There it was – our very own dinosaur fossil. We all crowded round for a good look.

"My oh my," said a little voice. "I wish it had been that easy for me."

# Cross chat

Will frowned. "Who said that?"

"'Twas me, my love."

Lizzie strode across the room. "Someone's behind Mr Fossil's desk."

"Not behind it," said the voice. "On it."

Picking up a book, Lizzie said, "This is all that's on – *woh*!" She dropped the book, then hurriedly picked it up, brushing it down. "Sorry!"

"'Tis all right, my love," said the voice. "Just stand me up, will 'ee?"

Lizzie stood the book on the desk. It fell open on a portrait of a woman in old-fashioned clothes, sitting on a rock. She jumped down and stepped out of the book on to the desk.

MARY ANNING'S MY NAME. I WAS THE FIRST PROPER COLLECTOR OF FOSSILS, MY WORD, YES. PROFESSIONAL COLLECTOR, THAT IS.

I LIVED IN LYME REGIS IN THE EARLY 19TH CENTURY. 'TWAS JUST A LITTLE SEASIDE TOWN, BUT IT BECAME WELL KNOWN TO FOLKS FROM LONDON AND IMPORTANT UNIVERSITIES — AND ALL 'COS OF ME.

THE CLIFFS AT LYME ARE FILLED WITH FOSSILS — EASY FOR ME TO DIG OUT. THOSE CLEVER MEN COULDN'T GET ENOUGH OF THE WONDERFUL THINGS I FOUND FOR THEM.

I KNOWS THAT YOUR MR FOSSIL SHOWED YOU A PLESIOSAUR. I, MY LOVES, DID FIND THE VERY FIRST PLESIOSAUR FOSSIL. AND THE FIRST PTERODACTYL. THERE! WHAT DO 'EE THINK OF THAT?

I reached out to touch Mary's hammer, but she pulled it back sharply. "Don't you touch that, my lad. 'Tis the tool of my trade!" Then she said, "Farewell," and stepped back into her book. Once she was back on her rock, you would never know she'd ever moved.

Mr Fossil closed the book. "Mary used that hammer to dig out fossils from the softer rocks, and fossil-hunters today use one much like it. Mind, you'd need more than a small hammer to get at some of the fossils that palaeontologists have found in harder rock."

"Pally who?" Arnie said.

Mr Fossil went over to the board and wrote:

PALAEONTOLOGIST
say PALLY-ON-TOL-OH-JIST

"Well, now we know how to say it," said Hiroko, cheekily, "but we don't know what it is."

"I do," I said.

Tess's eyes twinkled. "Had another book for breakfast, Gordon?" she asked.

I was about to stick my tongue out, when Mr Fossil said, "Tell us, then, Gordon."

I said, "A palaeontologist is someone who studies fossils."

"They're the clever people who've discovered what we know about so many dinosaurs," said Mr Fossil, looking more and more excited. What was he planning now?

"In the cupboard, everyone," he ordered.

"No way," said Will. "That bird's in there, and it's got teeth, remember."

Lizzie shoved him aside. "No pathetic little Archaeopteryx is going to scare me," she said. (True.) She opened the door and went in. Next second, she stuck her head out and said, "You'll never believe this…"

We swarmed in behind her.

78

"Such impertinence!" said a voice.

"Quite right," said another. "In my opinion, children should be seen and not– "

"Take no notice, 5F!" A young man with a "Gallery Attendant" badge hurried towards us. "They have rather old-fashioned ideas. Not surprising, really," he added. "Welcome to the gallery. Come and meet some of the residents."

"He's barmy," Tess whispered. But she slipped behind me when the attendant looked round, and he thought it was me who'd said it.

"*If* we're ready," he said, indicating a painting, "may I introduce Dr Mantell. He was the– "

The man in the painting turned his head. "Thank you, I will speak for myself."

"Funder wool!" said Mr Fossil.

"Wonderful," I whispered to Lizzie.

"I know," she said, "I'm not daft."

BUT YOU ARE INTERRUPTING! BEFORE I MADE MY WORK PUBLIC, PEOPLE NEVER SUSPECTED THAT GIANT REPTILES ONCE ROAMED THE EARTH. WHAT CHANGED EVERYTHING WAS MY DISCOVERY IN 1822 OF THE DINOSAUR I NAMED IGUANODON, NOT TO MENTION MY YEARS AND YEARS OF WORKING NIGHT AND DAY TO LEARN MORE ABOUT IT.

"Thank you, Dr Mantell," said Mr Fossil. "We'll find out more about the Iguanodon for homework."

Don't you just love that "we"? When did teachers ever do homework?

# ·DINOFAX·

## IGUANODON by Gordon

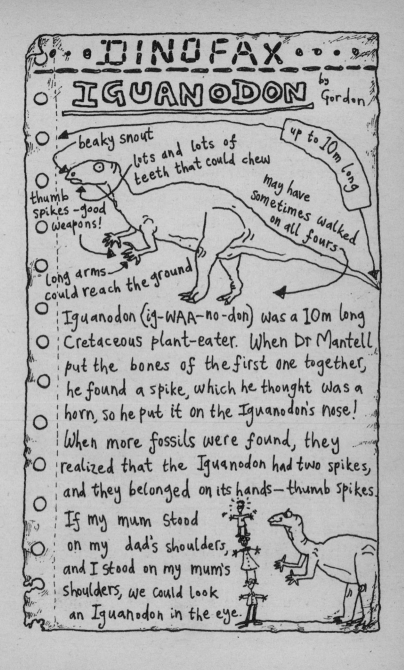

- beaky snout
- lots and lots of teeth that could chew
- up to 10m long
- may have sometimes walked on all fours
- thumb spikes - good weapons!
- long arms could reach the ground

Iguanodon (ig-WAA-no-don) was a 10m long Cretaceous plant-eater. When Dr Mantell put the bones of the first one together, he found a spike, which he thought was a horn, so he put it on the Iguanodon's nose!

When more fossils were found, they realized that the Iguanodon had two spikes, and they belonged on its hands—thumb spikes.

If my mum stood on my dad's shoulders, and I stood on my mum's shoulders, we could look an Iguanodon in the eye.

The attendant pointed to another portrait. "This is Sir Richard Owen." He tapped the frame. "Sir Richard?"

The man jumped. "What? What! Who is it?"

"Class 5F, Sir Richard," said the attendant. "They want to find out about your dinosaurs."

GOOD EH?

"DINOSAUR" MEANS "TERRIBLE LIZARD"

MANTELL DIDN'T KNOW WHAT A DINOSAUR WAS WHEN HE FOUND HIS IGUANODON. THE WORD DIDN'T EXIST UNTIL I INVENTED IT. I'M THE MAN WHO GAVE THESE CREATURES THEIR SPECIAL NAME.

I MADE A MOST INTELLIGENT GUESS AT WHAT THEY LOOKED LIKE, AND DESIGNED SOME SUPERB MODELS FOR THE GREAT EXHIBITION AT CRYSTAL PALACE.

QUEEN VICTORIA, GOD BLESS HER, CAME TO SEE THEM, Y'KNOW. THEY WEREN'T LITTLE MODELS BUT LIFE-SIZED WORKS OF ART. JOLLY FINE.

HAD A DINNER-PARTY INSIDE THE IGUANODON! HA HA!

THE INVITATIONS WERE WRITTEN ON A PTERO-DACTYL'S WING – NOT A REAL ONE – IT WAS ON PAPER, OF COURSE. MY, MY, WE HAD A FEW DRINKS THAT NIGHT, I CAN TELL YOU...

DINNER IN THE IGUANODON

"What's that noise?" I asked Arnie. "I can hear voices."

"Not surprising," said Arnie, "Owen's talking. Still."

"No, over there."

Arnie didn't even bother to look. "I expect you're going mad," he said, kindly.

Lucy Lee asked Sir Richard if dinosaurs were only discovered in England.

"Not at all," he said. "In fact, strange bones had been discovered long before we Victorians made our discoveries, but people thought they must be from giant humans, or dragons."

Knock, knock…

"Indeed," Mr Fossil said. "And America is a very happy hunting ground for today's palaeontologists."

Knock, knock, knock…

I looked round and saw something that made my mouth fall open (my mum says I look gormless when I do that and, since Tess came to my house, so does everyone else). A man in a painting further down the gallery was reaching *out* of the frame and knocking on the wall beside it.

"Ah!" said the attendant. "Someone wants our attention. Yes, Mr Cope?"

The man in the picture grasped his lapels, and announced, "I was the most famous and successful palaeontologist of my day, yes, sirree."

"Oh, no you weren't, Edward Drinker Cope. I was."

Eh? Who said that?

Mr Cope continued. "I was a university professor in the good old US of A."

The voice spoke again. "So was I – at *Yale*!"

That was too much for Mr Cope. He turned towards the next picture along, and snapped, "Of course you were, Othniel Marsh! Your family poured money into the darned place!"

"How dare you!"

The attendant stepped in. "Gentlemen, gentlemen!"

Lizzie snorted. "More like a pair of spitting cats than gentlemen!"

"Why not discuss this as old friends," said Mr Fossil. "After all, you *were* once friends before you started warring over your dinosaur finds. Come on, step down."

I'm not kidding, that's exactly what they did. First one leg, then the other and, as they turned from drawings into real flesh and blood, they grew until they were standing before us – just as if we'd gone back to America in the 19th century.

86

Again and again they stabbed each other with stiffly pointed fingers, until Mr Fossil stepped in.

"Gentlemen, enough," he said. "5F, let's go." He headed for the exit.

"Hey!" yelled Cope. "What about my Dystrophaeus? My Diclonius? My Tichosteus?"

Honestly, even Hiroko and Meena could have taken lessons in squabbling from those two.

"I'll leave them for a bit," said the attendant. "They like a good argument. The trouble is, you see, that palaeontologists are always finding new things." He opened the door. "And sometimes one tiny discovery can change the whole way we look at something."

"That's what makes it all so thrilling," said Mr Fossil. "When we add new information to what we know already, it sometimes shows our thinking has been wrong."

"Which *can* cause trouble." The attendant jerked his thumb at Marsh and Cope. "They're quite old, you know. They'll soon wear themselves out."

"Mr Fossil's very old," I said, "and he never gets tired."

"Ah," said the attendant, "but he's different."

You're telling me.

# Dig this!

On Thursday, Mr Fossil came in wearing strong walking boots. "We're off to meet one of today's palaeontologists," he said. "You'll find her more civil than Cope and Marsh. Everyone got boots on?"

Need he ask? I don't know how, I don't know when, but suddenly we all had boots on, just like his.

Mr Fossil unrolled a giant poster and fixed it to the wall.

"A picture of a door?" said Hiroko. "What use is that?"

We soon saw. Mr Fossil reached for the handle, opened the door and walked through.

The door closed behind him. Tess was first to move. You should have seen her face when she found she could actually get hold of the handle, too!

She opened it, stuck her head through, then looked back. "Get a load of this!"

Will groaned, but we trusted Mr Fossil, so we followed Tess through.

We found ourselves in bare, rocky country. In fact, there wasn't much to see apart from a few people hunched down on the ground and, when I looked back, I saw we'd just stepped out of a caravan.

"That's my home for a few months," said a woman in filthy jeans.

I'M MEL, AND I'M EXCAVATING A DINOSAUR.

"Hey!" She bounded over a rock and yanked Tess back. "Watch where you walk. Dino bones are very fragile, especially the skulls, and I hope to find a good one here. Come and see."

I'VE TAKEN OFF AS MUCH ROCK AS I CAN FROM ABOVE THIS PIECE OF LEG BONE, AND NOW I'M DIGGING IT AWAY AS FAR AS I CAN UNDERNEATH, THEN WE'LL BANDAGE AND PLASTER THE LEG TO MAKE SURE IT DOESN'T BREAK APART.

"That's what they did to my leg when I fell downstairs and broke it," I said.

Nita gripped my arm. "Don't fall over now," she said, "or you might break Mel's leg."

Hiroko was poking around. "Are these your tools?" she asked.

Mel nodded. "All those – and we use pneumatic drills sometimes, like road-menders, and even explosives."

91

# Handy Equipment for Fossil Hunters

Hammer

Chisel

Trowel

Compass, for working out where things are (and for finding your way home).

Notebook and pen, for writing down all about your find.

Paintbrush, for brushing off loose rock from bones.

Camera, to take snaps of the position of your fossil.

Toothbrush

Sandwiches, for hungry fossil hunters.

Goggles, to keep dust and chips of rock out of your eyes.

Hard hat, for protection against falling rocks and ~~dropping birds~~ bird droppings.

by Tess Taylor

"What sort of dinosaur is it?" Freddie asked.

"We don't know yet," said Mel. "We can see lots of fragments of bone, but this is the first large one we've got out. When it gets to the lab we'll find out more. What I'm really hoping is that it will turn out to be a magnificent specimen of Tyrannosaurus. Like Sue, only bigger."

"Who's Sue?"

Mel grinned. "There are two Sues. One is a palaeontologist, like me, and the other is the superb Tyrannosaurus rex she found. It was named after her. Hang on a sec." She ran to the caravan, and returned with a photo. "Here's a picture of what Sue might have looked like when it was alive."

"You mean 'she'," said Hiroko.

"I don't," said Mel. "It's not been possible to say for sure what sex Sue is. But there's lots I can tell you about it."

"Listen well," said Mr Fossil, "because I'll be expecting a T. rex Dinofax from one of you."

As Mel talked, we listened in silence until she pointed out its tiny arms. "If the T. rex fell over while it was running, it was in dead trouble. These little arms couldn't save it, so it was likely to fall flat on its face."

Everyone laughed. "Just like Gordon!"

Mel said I could keep the picture, which shut them up, and Mr Fossil said in that case, I could do the T. rex Dinofax.

# TYRANNO

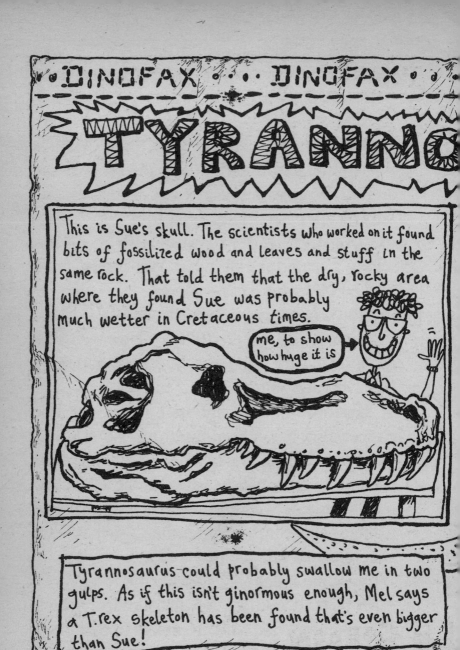

This is Sue's skull. The scientists who worked on it found bits of fossilized wood and leaves and stuff in the same rock. That told them that the dry, rocky area where they found Sue was probably much wetter in Cretaceous times.

me, to show how huge it is

Tyrannosaurus could probably swallow me in two gulps. As if this isn't ginormous enough, Mel says a T. rex skeleton has been found that's even bigger than Sue!

# SAURUS

Tyrannosaurus means "tyrant lizard"

over 12m long, as long as our school bus!

weighs about 7 tons

head 1·5m long (as long as our art tables)

massive jaws, 60 teeth up to 18cm long (like a bread knife blade)

small hands, with two fingers

1·25m from ankle to tip of claw

by GORDON

95

Mel didn't want to go back to the laboratory with her bone. She wanted to excavate more bones, and maybe teeth.

"All these fragments, however tiny, must be collected," she said, "because every little bit is a clue."

"Like a treasure hunt," said Penny.

"Just like one. We even make a map!"

"A map?" said Hiroko. "Don't you know where you are?"

THE MAP SHOWS THE EXACT POSITION OF EVERYTHING WE FIND AND THOSE DETAILS PROVIDE US WITH MORE CLUES ABOUT HOW THE DINOSAUR LIVED.

AND DIED!

"Exactly," said Mel. "The death of a dinosaur can give clues about where it lived, whether it was attacked – and what attacked it – and, if we find fossilized stomach contents, what it had for its last dinner."

"I hope it was a chunk of its murderer!" said Lizzie.

Soon Nita and Meena were helping Mel with the plastering.

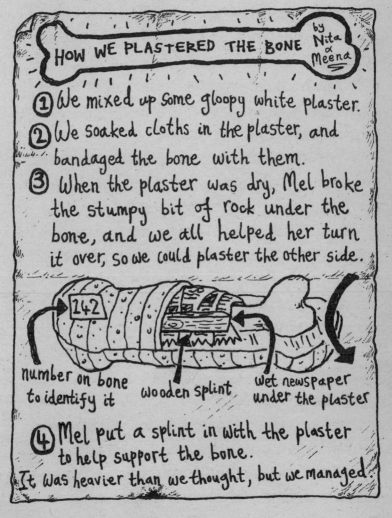

HOW WE PLASTERED THE BONE *by Nita & Meena*

1. We mixed up some gloopy white plaster.
2. We soaked cloths in the plaster, and bandaged the bone with them.
3. When the plaster was dry, Mel broke the stumpy bit of rock under the bone, and we all helped her turn it over, so we could plaster the other side.

number on bone to identify it

wooden splint

wet newspaper under the plaster

4. Mel put a splint in with the plaster to help support the bone.

It was heavier than we thought, but we managed

Nita and Meena had a lovely time, till they started flicking dollops of plaster at each other, and Mel got mad.

"Don't play around," she said crossly. "You're making me nervous – you might break something important."

When the second lot of plaster was almost dry, a cloud of dust appeared in the distance.

"Truck's coming," Mel said.

The dust cloud grew as it came nearer. The driver waved, turned in a big circle, and backed up as close to the bone as Mel would let him. She didn't want those big wheels crushing anything.

"Hi, Mel. Hi, kids. Hi, Archie," he said. "Plaster dry?"

Archie Fossil!

"Bet he's Archibald," Meena whispered.

Hiroko giggled. "Bald Archie! It suits him!"

That set me off, but I soon stopped laughing when I helped lift the bone on to the truck.

Heavy or what! I think the driver must have been pretty glad we were there.

"Phew!" The driver had a swig of water. "I'm off to the lab," he said, giving me a wink. "Be seeing you. Enjoy the eggs!"

He drove off, sending up a massive dust cloud. We couldn't see a thing at first, but when it cleared, we were back in class.

I suddenly realized that everyone was staring at me.

"Gordon, close your mouth. You're looking gormless," said Tess.

I made a face at her. "The driver said something about eggs," I said.

Mr Fossil clapped a hand to his forehead. "I clean forgot."

Then he did something I've never seen a teacher do in my life. He climbed on his desk!

"Well?" he said. "Up you get, everyone."

# Herd-watching

The fuss everyone made getting on their desks! Will tried to get on Nita's because it was by the wall. He felt safer there. Nita didn't want anyone near her desk for some reason. (Probably got a lifetime supply of Choco Bars in there.) Penny complained that heights made her dizzy, so Carrie insisted on climbing on with her.

"Stop muttering, everyone," said Mr Fossil, "and link hands."

I got Will and Nita's hands. Nita's was sticky.

Mr Fossil said, "Let's put out the light."

I don't know how he did it, but suddenly everything went dark. Black dark. In the middle of the day!

The whole class went quiet. I knew Will would be twitching, so I put a hand on his shoulder.

"Don't!" he said. "I know what you're like, Gordon. If you fall, you'll pull me down, too."

"Look up," said Mr Fossil.

A bright full moon came out from behind the clouds.

Eh? Clouds … moon…? In our classroom?

With a shock, we realized we weren't on our desks any more.

Way down below, lit by brilliant moonlight, was the forest floor.

"What are we doing here?" asked Tess.

Mr Fossil stabbed a bony finger towards the ground. "Looking at eggs."

"Wow!" said Lizzie. "That nest's the same shape as a volcano crater."

I leaned forward, "I'll just see if– "

"NO, GORDON!" everybody shouted.

Mr Fossil stood me back against the trunk. "Be careful," he warned. "There are dinosaurs below. Lots of dinosaurs."

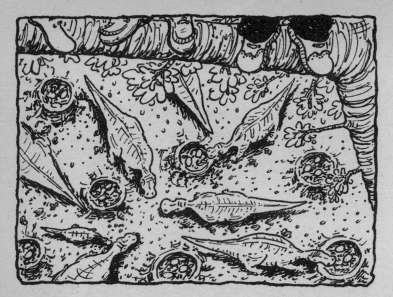

Everyone realized at the same time that there was not just one nest down there – there were loads! And loads of dinosaurs, too.

"They're called Maiasaura," said Mr Fossil.

DINOFAX

Maiasaura by Hiroko
(we say 'my-a-SORE-a")

rows of teeth in her cheeks

toothless beak

bony lump between the eyes

about 9m long

102

Scientists must have been surprised to discover a dino that looked after her babies so carefully. Maybe that's why they called her Maiasaura — it means "good mother lizard".

Maiasaura's nest

eggs

twigs and leaves

A Maiasaura's nest was about 2m across. She arranged her eggs carefully and covered them with twigs and leaves to keep them warm. (I suppose if she'd sat on them, like a hen, she'd have had scrambled eggs.) The new babies were about 30 cm long but by the time they left the nest they were five times as long. The mother fed them on leaves and berries. They grew quickly because they did nothing except eat. (Suit Nita!)

We watched the dinosaurs for a while. They were amazingly gentle for such big animals.

"Why are there so many all together?" I asked.

"Some plant-eaters moved in herds," said Mr Fossil. "Sometimes there were thousands and thousands of dinosaurs, all travelling together, moving on in search of food. And you can imagine what a benefit a herd was if a predator appeared."

"Yeah," said Arnie, "they could form a circle with the young ones in the middle, like in Wild West movies."

"You watch too much telly, Peasmarsh!" Carrie scoffed.

Mr Fossil smiled. "Arnie's right. What better way to protect their young than by forming a circle round them?"

"Cripes!" said Carrie. "If they put all the babies together, how would the mothers find the right ones afterwards? They're all identical."

"You might all be right," said Mr Fossil. "The truth is that we don't know for sure. Palaeontologists are finding new information all the time. For instance, let me tell you about the Oviraptor. Its name means 'egg thief', and I remember, many years ago– "

"You mean in the nineteenth century, sir?" Hiroko asked, with her best innocent expression. He fell for it.

"Well, let me see – was it then? Or after … or before?"

"Before!" whispered Nita. "How old can he *be*?"

He started counting on his fingers. "Ah! I remember now! It was in the 1920s. A fossilized skeleton of Oviraptor was found, and it seemed that it died in the act of stealing another dinosaur's eggs. That's how it got its name. Then, 70 years later, another Oviraptor fossil was found in a similar position. And you'll never guess! The Oviraptor was actually sitting on its own eggs, proving that it was probably a pretty good mother after all!"

Mr Fossil grinned round at us. "Fascinating, isn't it! Straight guff!

Meena looked at me, confused.

I whispered, "He means 'great stuff'."

"If by 'he' you mean me," said Mr Fossil, "that's what I said."

He must be years older than my gran, but he can hear better than I can.

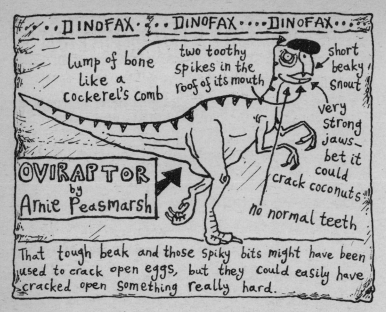

DINOFAX · DINOFAX · DINOFAX

lump of bone like a cockerel's comb

two toothy spikes in the roof of its mouth

short beaky snout

very strong jaws – bet it could crack coconuts

OVIRAPTOR by Arnie Peasmarsh

no normal teeth

That tough beak and those spiky bits might have been used to crack open eggs, but they could easily have cracked open something really hard.

"Were all nests the same?" asked Hiroko. "Did all dinosaurs look after their babies like Maiasaura?"

"That will make a good topic for homework," said Mr Fossil. "Speaking of which, it's time you were there."

"Where?"

"Home."

And with that, the moon vanished behind a cloud, everything went black, then light returned – and we were back on our desks.

"Soon be tea-time," Nita said happily. "Scrambled eggs, I think."

# EGGY INFORMATION

Some eggs were round, some oval, some sausage-shaped and some looked like potatoes. Some were small and some were like footballs! by Tess.

Some dinosaurs dug holes in the ground and laid their eggs in a circle or spiral, all pointing the same way. Neat.
by Meena.

Some giant plant-eaters' eggs were 30cm long. That's twice the size of an ostrich egg! They laid them in a row. Maybe they did it as they walked along...

They must have had pretty tough shells! by Freddie.

Some baby dinosaurs left the nest straight away to go hunting for food, but they stayed close to the adults.
by Nita

which way to the best nosh?

# Bones, horns and frilly bits

As we went in after break on Friday, Mr Fossil stood at the classroom door and handed each of us a piece of card.

Mine was a yellow rectangle – and completely blank.

"What's this?" asked Hiroko.

"Tickets," said Mr Fossil.

"Don't be daft," she said. "They're blank, so how can…" Her voice trailed off.

Hiroko must have seen the same thing as me – black letters forming on my ticket. Soon, they were clear enough to read.

When we looked up, that's where we were! The museum!

A young woman met us. "Good morning!" she said. "I'm Sarah. Your bone's arrived!"

We went into a long room. People were hunched over benches all down both sides. They were concentrating so hard that no one looked up from their work.

Our bone was on a sturdy table, and a man was snipping away the last bits of plaster.

"This is Peter," said Sarah. "He's a preparator, and his job is to take bones like this and clean them up, so they can be properly examined and put on display."

"When you get some bones, how can you tell what dinosaur they're from?" I asked.

"Good question," Peter said. "It's like detective work. We can compare bones with other skeletons and see if it's from one we already know about. Marks on bones tell us where muscles and ligaments went, so we can work out how the dinosaur moved, and what it might have looked like. Holes in its skull tell us how big its brain and eyes were –"

"And teeth tell you what it ate," added Tess.

"All those clues help us to identify it," said Peter, "or even to know if we have a new type of dinosaur. That could happen any day, because we certainly haven't found all there is to find. That's what makes my job so exciting. But first, we have to actually get at the bone, and that means removing the rock from around it. Come and see some of our equipment."

Peter steered us towards a contraption called a shot-blaster. He put his hands inside, through two holes that ended in gloves, and picked up a lump of rock.

"There's a fossil inside this," he said, and pointed a tube at the rock. Suddenly the tank filled with what looked like dust, and there was a noise like a hailstorm!

"This is a great way to clean off a thick layer of rock," he shouted.

Hiroko tapped him on the arm. He switched off the machine a split-second before she bellowed, "IT'S TOO NOISY!"

"It's not," Meena giggled. "You are!"

Sarah introduced us to another technician who was working on our bone with a hammer and chisel.

"This is too big to go in the shot-blaster," he said. "It's still got lots of rock stuck to it, though, especially this big lump. Who wants to help?"

Everybody did, of course, so we only had a quick go. I put the edge of the chisel against the rock part, hammered the handle and chipped away some little chunks. We weren't allowed to go anywhere *near* where the bone was. That's only for experts.

Then Sarah showed us how to use a special chisel, powered by air, to carefully remove the last rock particles from a knuckle bone. It was really noisy, and we had to stand well back, because minute rock grains spat all over her table.

I was just wishing I could have a go, when Sarah said, "Would somebody like to –"

"Me!" I pushed forward, tripped over my own stupid feet and fell flat on the floor.

"– pass me a tissue," she finished, as I lay nose down in the dust. "I'm going to sneeze."

Tess, who always had the sneezes, stuffed a tissue in her hand, then reached down to pull me up. As I got to my knees, I noticed a bone lying on the floor.

I would have handed it over, but Will called everyone to look at a ghastly claw he'd spotted on a bench. I suppose I slipped the bone into my pocket without thinking.

"That's mind-boggling!" said Tess. "Just think – that was once part of a living animal."

Sarah coughed. "Well, actually, it wasn't," she said. "It's a replica."

"A what?" I asked.

A REPLICA IS AN EXACT COPY OF THE REAL THING. IF PEOPLE SHOW US SOMETHING TRULY RARE, WE ASK THEM TO GIVE IT, OR LEND IT, TO THE MUSEUM. WE MAKE THEM A REPLICA OF THEIR FIND TO KEEP AT HOME TO SHOW THEIR FRIENDS. THE MORE DINOSAUR REMAINS WE SCIENTISTS CAN STUDY, THE MORE WE DISCOVER.

I'VE SEEN ENOUGH OF THIS ONE!

We were allowed to wander round the museum and make notes for our Dinofax book. It was brilliant! We were the only visitors, so we could see everything without having our eyes poked out by someone's backpack. Mr Fossil loved it! He bounced around saying things like, "Dot a way!"

I liked the way dinosaurs from one family were all grouped together. You could see that, even though they were related, there were differences, like with Triceratops. That was one dinosaur we recognized, because of the "tri" in its name. "Tri" means three, like in tricycle, and triangle, so I guessed that Triceratops meant "three-horn". Its head was huge – about a third of its whole length!

THIS CHAP'S ALMOST AS LONG AS THREE CAMELS NOSE-TO-TAIL, AND I RECKON IT WEIGHS AS MUCH AS TWO ELEPHANTS! THAT SHIELD OVER ITS NECK IS GREAT PROTECTION. IT'S A SOLID SHEET OF BONE. IMAGINE BEING CHARGED BY THOSE HORNS!

Meena and Hiroko got a bit silly round the Pachyrhinosaurus, prancing around pretending to be scared, and calling it a rhino-dino.

# PACHYRHINOSAURUS

## by Arnie Peasmarsh.

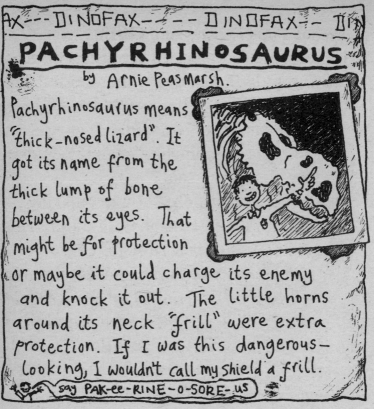

Pachyrhinosaurus means "thick-nosed lizard". It got its name from the thick lump of bone between its eyes. That might be for protection or maybe it could charge its enemy and knock it out. The little horns around its neck "frill" were extra protection. If I was this dangerous-looking, I wouldn't call my shield a frill.

say PAK-ee-RINE-O-SORE-us

"Hey! Why are some of this dinosaur's bones a different colour?" Arnie asked.

"Try reading the label," said Tess.

We looked over Arnie's shoulder.

This skeleton isn't complete. Experts have used fibreglass to make the missing parts, so it can be displayed for you to see. The lighter-coloured bones are real ones.

"What's that?" squeaked Carrie.

I'd heard it, too. It sounded like distant thunder.

Nita giggled. "Sorry," she said. "My tummy's rumbling. Where's Old Fossil?"

"Right behind you," he said.

"Oops!" Nita gave him her "charming" smile. "It's lunchtime," she said.

He checked his watch. "You're amazing."

You don't need clocks with Nita. Her stomach knows the exact time of day.

We said goodbye to Sarah and left through the door marked "Way out". Perhaps it should have said "Way in", because we found ourselves back in our classroom!

"Hang on," said Freddie. "All those dinosaurs were pretty tough, right?"

"Right," said Mr Fossil.

"If they were so tough, how come they're not around any more?"

"That," said Mr Fossil, "is exactly what we're going to find out after lunch." He frowned. "At least, we'll try to find out."

We looked at each other. Try? Didn't he know?

# Way to go!

On the way back from lunch, I felt in my pocket for a sweet.

Flip! I still had that bone – the one I found on the museum floor. Oh well, too late now. I cheered up when I thought how good it would look on the shelf at home.

Nita started sounding off as soon as we got in class. "I bet I know why dinosaurs died out," she said. "Earth was invaded by aliens, and they forgot to bring any food, so they ate all the dinosaurs."

"That's stupid," Will said.

MAYBE THEY GOT A DREADFUL DISEASE AND DIED IN AGONY WITH THEIR TONGUES STICKING OUT.

YUK!

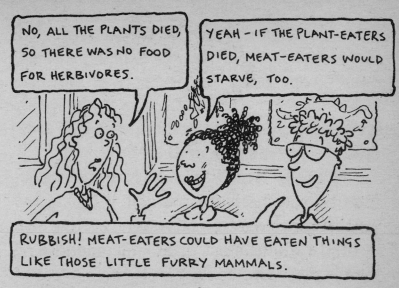

NO, ALL THE PLANTS DIED, SO THERE WAS NO FOOD FOR HERBIVORES.

YEAH – IF THE PLANT-EATERS DIED, MEAT-EATERS WOULD STARVE, TOO.

RUBBISH! MEAT-EATERS COULD HAVE EATEN THINGS LIKE THOSE LITTLE FURRY MAMMALS.

Hiroko asked, "What do you think, Fister Mossil?"

Meena spluttered into her hand, and the rest of us could hardly keep our faces straight, but he never even noticed!

"Believe it or not, all your ideas have been suggested over the years," he said, "and there are many even wilder ideas."

"Like what?" asked Freddie.

"One theory was that the dinosaurs committed suicide by jumping off cliffs! Another was that the fumes from all that dino dung suffocated them."

Meena giggled. "Death by poo!"

Mr Fossil ignored that. "Someone suggested that mammals ate all the dinosaur eggs, so no babies were born. And there was the daft radiation theory – deadly rays from space were supposed to have hit Earth, but they didn't quite reach the ground."

"That makes sense," I said. "It explains why little animals didn't die out."

"So?" Freddie spread his hands. "How can we find out what happened to the dinosaurs?"

"Ask one," Hiroko said.

"One what?" said Meena.

"A dinosaur, of course."

"Don't be stupid," said Tess. "We need an expert."

"Quite right," said Mr Fossil. "Gordon, go to the computer and do a search."

Everyone rushed to pull their feet and bags out of my way. I clicked on Gogettit, our favourite search engine. I typed in *Why did dinosaurs die out?* and clicked the Gogettit icon.

The first website it suggested was www.prof.windrush.ed.

"Professor Windrush!" said Mr Fossil. "Perfect! Gogettit, Gordon!"

I downloaded the site.

If ever anyone had the wrong name, it was Professor Windrush. His arms waved around so wildly he should have been called Professor Windmill.

He leaned forward, almost as if he could see us.

GOOD AFTER- NOON, 5F!

He *could* see us!

The Professor waved, knocking a pencil pot off a shelf, then cupped his ear. "Can't hear you."

I was too surprised to speak!

"Hi, Professor," said Lizzie. A few of us muttered, "Hello."

He threw his hands wide. "Welcome!" A row of books crashed to the floor.

"He's worse than you, Gordon," said Arnie.

"Quiet, Peasmarsh," said the Professor,

which cheered me up. "You want to know what happened to the dinosaurs, yes?"

"Yes!"

"The simple answer," said Professor Windrush, "is – we don't know. But," he added, "we have some very good ideas. Number one!"

Whoosh! A bright light shot across his study.

The professor's whole room shook, and I swear the ground shook under our feet, too!

"Wh-what was that?" Will squeaked.

"A meteorite strike," said Professor Windrush. "Take a look."

He held the globe up for us to see. There was a huge circular dent, just near Mexico.

"What a massive crater," said Freddie.

"Did that really happen?" asked Tess. "A meteorite from space?"

WE KNOW THAT EARTH SUDDENLY COOLED DOWN AROUND 65 MILLION YEARS AGO, WHICH IS WHEN THE DINOSAURS DIED OUT. THAT METEORITE COULD HAVE BEEN THE CAUSE.

THERE'S A CRATER BURIED DEEP OFF THE COAST OF MEXICO, AND WE BELIEVE IT MEASURES MORE THAN 180 KM FROM EDGE TO EDGE — MAYBE AS MUCH AS 300 KM! THE METEOR THAT CAUSED IT WAS PROBABLY BETWEEN 10 KM AND 15 KM ACROSS. THAT'S A MIGHTY BIG CHUNK OF ROCK!

Penny frowned. "How could that have cooled the Earth?"

"The meteorite would have exploded – ker-*boom*!" The Professor slipped off his desk and tottered upright. "Actually, it would have been a thousand ker-booms all at once. Like this –"

"All the debris thrown up into the Earth's atmosphere would have blotted out the sun," he continued. "And without sunlight– "

"Plants would die," I said.

"And if plants die," said Tess, "the creatures that eat them would die."

"Bright kids!" said the Professor. "I'll show you what *might* have happened. Click 'Print', please."

Carrie was nearest. She clicked. Instantly, pictures began whizzing out of the printer.

Meteorite hits — like thousands of nuclear bombs going off all at once! Shock waves cause volcanoes to erupt, earthquakes, hurricanes, landslides and tidal waves. Millions of tons of dust and water vapour blast into Earth's atmosphere. Sun's blotted out. Sky dark. Earth is co-o-old.

This is like the worst disaster movie!

Plants die. Animals small enough to burrow escape the worst of the cold.

*There's some desperate plant-eaters here.*

Plant-eaters die. Scavenging meat-eaters feed off them.

*Now we have some very dead plant-eaters. Dead of starvation.*

When herbivores are gone, carnivores starve to death. Small mammals feed off their carcasses.

*Yeah! Mammals are hanging in there!*

Sun reappears. Plants shoot. Mammals survive. Earth warms and the world begins to live again.

But it's a world without dinosaurs.

"So mammals were the only survivors?" said Lucy Lee.

"That's part of the mystery," said the Professor. "They weren't! Birds survived, and so did crocodiles and other reptiles, like lizards and snakes. Frogs, too."

"Weird!" said Nita. "You'd have expected huge, tough dinos to survive anything."

Tess ruffled her hair. "It seems to me," she said slowly, "that the ones who lasted out until things got better again were the smaller ones."

"Absolutely!" The Professor punched the air, sending his lampshade swinging. "Smart girl!"

Tess went bright red, and we all stuck our fingers in our mouths and made being-sick faces. Especially me, because I was the one who pointed out about little creatures surviving, when we heard the deadly space rays theory.

Mr Fossil asked, "Do you believe the meteorite strike caused the dinosaurs to die out, Professor?"

"Some days I do, and some days I don't," was the reply. "There's always the volcano theory. Take a look!"

A new window opened on screen.

SOME PEOPLE BELIEVE THAT EARTH MOVEMENTS CAUSED LOTS OF VOLCANOES TO ERUPT. THE SUN WOULD HAVE BEEN BLOCKED OUT BY THOUSANDS OF TONS OF DUST, CHUNKS OF ROCK, AND ASH BLASTED INTO THE AIR, AND THERE WOULD HAVE BEEN FIRES...

"Fires?" said Lucy.

A deep rumbling vibration filled my insides. The others felt it, too. We clutched our tummies.

"Of course, fires," said Professor Windrush, hanging on to his desk as the computer began to vibrate. "See?"

With a roar and a whoosh! the volcano erupted! Red fire spurted from the top of the computer and burning lava poured down the sides.

"It'll set us on fire!" shrieked Will.

"It will *not*," said Mr Fossil, and he blew – first on the volcano. The fire went out as easily as if he'd blown out candles on a birthday cake. Then he blew on the lava. It turned dark and hard.

Hiroko giggled nervously. "Did you make a wish?"

"I don't think I should say what I'm wishing right now," Mr Fossil said grimly. "Professor Windrush is very brainy, but he always goes over the top."

"Like the volcano," I said.

Mr Fossil laughed. "Exactly!" He turned to the computer. "Thank you, Professor, and goodbye."

"Wait," said the Professor. "There are lots more theories. Let me tell you– "

The screen went dark.

Freddie eyed the lumpy lava spread across the floor. "How are you going to explain that to the cleaners, sir?"

Mr Fossil looked mystified. "Explain what?"

Freddie pointed, then gaped.

The lava was gone.

THAT'S ENOUGH EXCITEMENT FOR ONE DAY.

I DON'T THINK SO!

# Video stars

Mr Fossil put on a peculiar pair of spectacles. Everyone laughed. One lens was red and the other green!

When we saw what else he had, we cheered. A video!

"Is it about dinosaurs?" asked Will.

"It is," said Mr Fossil. "And I shall be expecting some excellent homework tomorrow morning. Put these on."

He handed each of us a pair of the funny red and green specs. We put them on. The world looked very odd.

"Come to the TV," said Mr Fossil. "Don't worry about chairs."

"I'm not standing through a whole video," complained Meena.

"You are." Mr Fossil inserted the tape. "We won't need chairs where we're going."

Going?

The titles came up over a sideways view of a dinosaur. Suddenly it turned and roared at us. Will wasn't the only one to jump. It seemed to come right out of the screen at us.

The penny dropped.

I looked round. The others were still there, but instead of desks and shelves there were bushes, trees, insects – and warm sunshine.

We were actually *in* the movie!

"Keep together, everyone," said Mr Fossil. "Stay among these trees, and don't touch anything strange – that includes berries and fruits. We're back in the Mesozoic era, but you'll be quite safe as long as you don't actually touch anything." He crouched down and pointed. "Look!"

Just beyond the edge of the trees was what looked like a hosepipe. It moved. I followed the length of it with my eyes … it got thicker and thicker … and, with a gasp, I realized it was attached to a dinosaur's bottom. We were looking at a tail!

"Argentinosaurus is pretty big, too," said Mr Fossil, "but if you mean the longest, that's Seismosaurus. But then new discoveries are made all the time. By the way, I'm expecting some contributions for our Dinofax book."

"Bags this one, then," I said. I love those giant herbivores.

--- D I N O F A X ---

Mamenchisaurus was up to 22 m long.

# MAMENCHISAURUS

22m

That neck's half of the length of its whole body.

# ARGENTINOSAURUS

30m

Argentinosaurus was another herbivore, but even bigger — up to 30m! It probably weighed 50 tons — that's like 10 elephants!

# SEISMOSAURUS

40m

Seismosaurus was the biggest giant — up to 40m long, and all on a veggie diet. No wonder its name means "earth-shaking lizard". — by Gordon Budd

The giants never stopped eating, but with bodies that size to fill, I wasn't surprised.

"It's hard to believe creatures so big can be so gentle," said Meena.

"You wouldn't say that if one trod on you," said Hiroko.

"She wouldn't say much at all," said Lizzie. "She'd be squished!"

Tess asked confidently, "The biggest meat-eater is T. rex, right?"

"It's not," I said. "My dinosaur book says –"

"Just a sec," said Mr Fossil. He had the remote control! Z-i-i-p! The peaceful giants vanished and right in front of us was a group of tiny dinosaurs.

"They're so *cute*!" said Lizzie, going all gooey.

135

"Leave the Compys alone," said Mr Fossil. "They might be on the menu for some other dinosaur."

"Like what?" asked Hiroko.

LIKE THAT!

Yikes! When I saw what he meant, it took all my courage to stay still.

"Remember, nothing will hurt us if we don't touch it," said Mr Fossil.

"There's no way I'd even get within sniffing distance of that," said Meena. "Its mouth's dripping blood."

"Deinonychus is its name," said Mr Fossil. "It means 'terrible claw'. I imagine you can see why."

"I remember," said Lizzie. "It has that claw that can fold up out of the way when it runs."

I felt sick when I looked at Deinonychus's feet, and even sicker when three more of the monsters appeared.

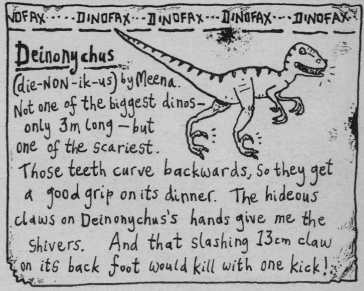

DINOFAX · · · DINOFAX · · DINOFAX · · · DINOFAX · · · DINOFAX

**Deinonychus**
(die-NON-ik-us) by Meena.
Not one of the biggest dinos —
only 3m long — but
one of the scariest.
Those teeth curve backwards, so they get
a good grip on its dinner. The hideous
claws on Deinonychus's hands give me the
shivers. And that slashing 13cm claw
on its back foot would kill with one kick!

Suddenly, the heads of the four Deinonychus snapped round and gazed, unblinking, at a small dinosaur, peacefully chomping on a bush. Stealthily they stalked it. I saw the killer claws pulled up and back. They broke into a run. I didn't want to watch, but I couldn't take my eyes off them. They were so fast!

Just before they pounced, Mr Fossil pressed the zapper.

Z-i-i-p! I blinked as the scene changed.

"Wow!" said Arnie, looking at an altogether different dinosaur. *"That's* got to be the biggest meat-eater ever."

"It's not," I said. "I keep telling you– "

"The biggest one's a T. rex," said Tess. "That's not a T. rex, is it, sir?"

"It's related," he said. "It's an Albertosaurus. This Cretaceous dinosaur might have been smaller than Tyrannosaurus but it had more of those nasty backward-pointing teeth with edges like a saw.

"Neither T. rex nor Albertosaurus is the biggest meat-eater," Mr Fossil went on. "That honour goes to the chap creeping up beyond those trees."

"Yikes!" said Will. It was the first word he'd uttered since we'd come into the movie.

Mr Fossil smiled. "How about you doing a Dinofax on that one, Will?"

DINOFAX · · · · · DINOFAX · · · DINOFAX

This huge horrible dinosaur lived in the Cretaceous period and it was at least 12·5m long! It probably weighed about 8 tons. I got jelly-legs just drawing this, so imagine what I felt like when I saw it. It's name means "giant southern lizard" and you say "JIG-an-OH-toe-SORE-us"

GIGANOTOSAURUS

by Will

"Lizzie! Remember to keep close together," Mr Fossil warned.

She and Hiroko might not be keeping close to the rest of us, but they were keeping *very* close to each other – as if they were hiding something. I edged round to have a look. No, it was just Lizzie's jacket, all balled up.

"There's another dinosaur that's not much smaller than Giganotosaurus," said Mr Fossil.

"If we've all looked enough here, let's fast forward to the duckbills. LIZZIE! HIROKO!" he bellowed. "Come back NOW!"

Lizzie's face was flushed. She looked very guilty, and kept behind Hiroko, clutching her jacket in her arms.

Z-i-i-p!

We found ourselves looking at the strangest dinosaurs we'd seen so far. Thousands of them!

"What on earth have they got on their heads?" I asked.

"Crests," said Mr Fossil. "Parasaurolophus belongs to a group of dinos called the duckbills. That crest is about as long as me! Scientists think that air travels up the back of it and down the front, and makes a trumpeting noise that Parasaurolophus uses to call to others – rather like a built-in hooter!"

Just when we thought we'd seen the strangest dinosaur ever, this one came on the scene…

We all, at the same time, became aware of another sound that almost drowned out the distant hooting of the Parasaurolophus herd – a ringing noise.

"What's that?" asked Meena.

"A dingdongosaurus," said Hiroko, and fell about laughing.

"It's the home bell," said Mr Fossil. "We'd better move. Don't take your specs off until I've stopped the video." He went to press the stop button, but glanced up at the sound of a muffled squeak.

"What was that?"

Everyone looked mystified – except one person, who went bright red.

Mr Fossil frowned. "Lizzie?"

She smiled, but it didn't work.

"What have you got inside that jacket?" Mr Fossil demanded.

"What jacket?"

"Lizzie," Mr Fossil said firmly. "Drop it."

Her mouth drooped. "Do I have to? It's so cute."

"DROP IT!"

Lizzie shook her jacket and out flopped – a Compsognathus!

Mr Fossil was bug-eyed. "Lizzie, have you gone round the bend?"

"I bet she wants it as a pet," I said.

"Yes. Thank you, Gordon," said Mr Fossil. He didn't sound all that grateful.

The Compy strutted around looking mean – hardly surprising after being scrunched up in Lizzie's jacket.

Will flapped. "It's a predator. It eats meat!"

He backed up against a tree. The Compy moved towards him. He was cornered.

"It'll bite me!" Will squealed.

"Nonsense," said Mr Fossil. "It only eats lizards and insects."

Will went white. "B-b-but there aren't any. The only meat around is – me!"

"Quick, someone," yelled Meena. "Throw it something."

"We haven't got anything," wailed Arnie.

I fished in my pockets, and my hand closed over the one thing that might attract the Compy's attention.

My bone.

I threw it. "Run, Will," I yelled. "Run *now*!"

And as the Compy darted at the bone, Will did the bravest thing he'd ever done.

We all yelled at Mr Fossil, "Stop the video!"
And he did. We were safe.

It was such a relief to take off the specs,
and to see the video credits running. Once
we'd got over the fright, everyone said how
fantastic it was to wander among dinosaurs.

"Nobody else in the whole world can do
that," said Nita.

"Just as well," muttered Will.

"What do you think of dinosaurs now?" Mr
Fossil asked.

"I can't wait for the next lesson," said Tess.

"That's a shame," said Mr Fossil, "because
this is our last one."

And do you know, even Will gave a little
groan. I think he deserves a medal.